Six-Word Lessons for

INTENTIONAL

PARENTING

100 Timeless Lessons to Help Your Kids Learn, Laugh and Love

Mary Waldmann

Published by Pacelli Publishing
Bellevue, Washington

Six-Word Lessons for Intentional Parenting

Published by Pacelli Publishing
9905 Lake Washington Blvd. NE, #D-103
Bellevue, Washington 98004
PacelliPublishing.com

Cover and interior designed by Pacelli Publishing
Author photo by Yuen Lui
Cover photo by Pixabay.com

ISBN-10: 1-933750-67-7
ISBN-13: 978-1-933750-67-5

Contents

Introduction

All parents want to raise happy, emotionally healthy and responsible kids. Doing a good job of parenting is always a challenge and I think it's particularly so in the twenty-first century. I had careers in several fields. They were interesting and stressful jobs, but I found my job as a parent to be the most challenging and the most stressful, and also the most satisfying and the most fun.

My husband and I believed that our primary parenting tasks were to love our children and to teach them responsibility and ethics, plus creativity, language and even science. This book details specific things we taught, from early ages, and how we did it. Many of these concepts were a result of how we were raised, as well as parenting books and articles, and advice from other parents. We also learned a lot through trial and error, and paid attention to what we wanted to repeat or avoid based on how we were raised.

Your most important teaching needs to be done from birth to ten years. After that, you're up against peer pressure, raging hormones and children's increasing efforts at independence. Things you do correctly in those first ten years can make eventual life with your teenagers much, much easier and will prepare them to be successful adults.

The success of your efforts won't fully be seen until your children reach adulthood. I'm happy to report that all three of our children have turned out to be happy, responsible, creative adults with interesting and successful careers. All three have found life partners whom we wholeheartedly embrace. Much of the credit belongs to them. They are all talented and have worked very hard to reach their success. But we also think the principles we taught as parents laid the groundwork for their happiness and success as adults.

In this book, I share tried-and-true wisdom that still works today, and things my husband Ray and I did that worked well for us. Kids and families are all unique and you'll want to tailor these tips to your particular child and family situation. Remember that "your mileage may vary," but I hope you'll find this advice helpful.

Acknowledgements

Many thanks to the generous people who read this book in draft form and gave me valuable suggestions: husband Raymond; children Elle Lake, John Waldmann and Emily Waldmann; the Rev. Karen Haig, mom, pastor and parenting coach; moms Carey Sheffield, Sunni Bannon and Tori Evans; and, of course, to my great editor and publisher, Patty Pacelli.

Dedication

This book is dedicated to my awesome children, Elle, John and Emily, who taught me so much about parenting in the course of their growing up and who continue to bring me great joy.

Rule Number One: Always Love Unconditionally

1

Love is essential to your child.

Children cannot thrive physically, emotionally or socially without lots of love and attention. And your child doesn't just need your love, she desperately wants it. Even kids who've been abused by a parent still struggle for that parent's love. We were lavish with our love and didn't require them to earn it in any way.

2

Be physically affectionate with your child.

Love is conveyed in many ways, but a key one is through touch. Babies who aren't handled don't thrive. From the time they were babies, we gave our children lots of holding, cuddle time, and physical playtime. We still give hugs and kisses to our adult children. They never outgrow their need for our physical affection.

3

Love is essential for self-esteem.

Your child's self-esteem is based almost solely on their relationship with you during the early years. Your love remains important even into adulthood. Bonding with you also makes them want to please you as they enter toddlerhood and helps them develop empathy for others, which is key to social and moral development.

4

Your child needs plenty of "face time."

Your face and voice are the first things your baby responds to and are essential for bonding. We were generous with it: nightly family dinners, holding them and talking, story time, family activities and even occasional "date nights" for an individual child with one parent. It remains important as they grow. An electronic screen is no substitute for parental interaction.

5

Never discipline kids by withholding love.

Never discipline your child by withholding your love. On occasion, my father gave me the silent treatment for misbehaving and it was devastating—I felt abandoned, unloved and unworthy. Even when they were in trouble, our kids always knew we loved them. No matter what she does, don't stop loving your child, even briefly. Let your love be unwavering.

6

Criticize actions but not your child.

Even when we were reprimanding our children, we never criticized them for who they were. I once observed my father-in-law tell our young son he was a "bad, bad boy" and I saw what a devastating effect it had on him. We corrected our children when necessary but we never challenged their essential goodness. Criticize behavior, not your child.

7

Be generous with approval and praise.

Kids need to know that you believe in their goodness. Tell them what you like about them. Praise them when they do something correctly or well. We were lavish in praising them and used it to reinforce good behavior and right choices. We let them hear us praise them to others. We are still generous with our praise.

8

Don't tell them they are perfect.

Don't praise your children if they don't deserve it and don't lead them to believe they're perfect kids. My husband's mother frequently told him he was a perfect child and better than any other. To this day, he gets frustrated and angry when he feels he's not perfect or others discount or critique his suggestions.

17

9

Respect your child's autonomy when appropriate.

Childhood is about gradually developing healthy autonomy. We wanted our kids to grow up to be independent, decisive adults so we let them make choices beginning with simple ones in toddlerhood. Choices grew as they did. Another mother once told me she "could tell" my kindergartner chose what to wear—I chose to take it as a compliment.

10

Your child will never be you.

Children like to hear how they resemble their parents in good ways. But don't expect him to be a "mini-me" or to live out your unfulfilled dreams. We cherished our children's differences and unique qualities. We recognized that their talents, interests and dreams frequently differed from ours and we respected those differences.

It's Your Job to Set Rules

11

Kids need limits for many reasons.

Obviously, kids need rules to keep them safe. They also need to learn the rules of social behavior, which are necessary if they're going to navigate the adult world successfully. Rules also help you impart ethics and develop conscience. Kids feel safer when there are limits. When peer pressure sets in, "My parents won't let me" is a helpful excuse.

12

Try to reinforce their positive behavior.

Praise your kids for their good behavior and choices. Your approval makes it more likely they'll do the same thing next time. Especially when a rule was new, we praised our kids when they followed it. Your child doesn't need a treat or any reward for doing the right thing. Your approval is all they really want.

13

Keep the rules appropriate for age.

Don't expect more of your child than she can deliver at her age. Toddlers can handle simple rules like "don't bite," "don't hit" and "don't scream." They can also learn basic manners, helping them navigate the social world as adults. We expected them to learn those lessons, but we didn't overtax their age or development. That sets up failure.

14

Explain the reason for your rules.

Children, like adults, are more likely to follow rules when they understand the "why," which is a question particularly popular with little ones! Is it for their safety, for getting along with others? Does it reflect a value that's important to you? When setting a rule, we explained it . . . and frequently had to explain it again!

15

Misbehavior will make a consequence necessary.

Simple offenses require only a reprimand, but we always felt that serious rule violations required further consequences. Sometimes an apology isn't enough. Consequences reinforce to your child in a lasting way why he should obey the rule. Major rule-breaking that has no consequences is much more likely to be repeated.

16

Make consequences fair and age-appropriate.

We tried to keep the consequences in line with the severity of the offense and they were never more than our children could handle. If the rule wasn't understood, we clarified it and a reprimand sufficed. If temper was involved, we discussed that. Knowing misbehavior warranted more serious measures, but we always kept them age-appropriate.

17

Never discipline when you are angry.

Disciplining a child when angry often leads to yelling and hitting, both bad things in child-rearing. I'll confess I yelled or swatted a few times and then felt ashamed of myself. What usually worked for me was telling my child, "I'm really angry right now, so you and I are both going to take a time-out until I cool down."

18

Make the consequences fit the behavior.

When my nine-year-old daughter, in trouble, fled to her bedroom, locked the door and refused to come out, I bided my time. When she finally came out, I, using chisel and hammer, removed her door from its hinges. It went into the garage and was earned back with two weeks of good behavior. The door was never locked again. Be creative!

19

Your child may help define consequences.

When our son was eight, he burst into tears and confessed he'd stolen candy bars from our neighbor. When I asked him what he thought we needed to do about it, he sobbed, "We need to call the police!" Not something I would have thought of, but knowing our small-town police, I called. It was just what he needed—and left a lasting impression.

20

Let him know he's still loved.

When the consequences have been imposed, forgive, forget and move on. I always tried to end a disciplinary talk with a hug. I wanted our children to be clear that there was nothing they could do that would cause them to lose our love. I think that's partially why they are such secure and loving adults.

Raise an Honest and Ethical Child

21

Moral values are necessary for children.

We wanted our kids to become honorable and ethical adults so we tried to impart those moral values as they grew. Young children seem to have an early sense of fair play. If you have more than one child you'll often hear, "That's not fair!" so teach them to be fair to others. The Golden Rule is basic to their moral grounding.

22

Ethics don't come naturally to children.

While they can understand fairness early, other moral values are harder. Children don't really develop any conscience until about age nine because it requires developing empathy, understanding of right versus wrong, and the ability to control their behavior. We tried to help them learn the right thing to do, while being patient with them.

23

Set an example with your actions.

If your child sees you shoplifting or hears you lying, he's bound to repeat that behavior. We set an example by what we did. I told them that when they didn't want to visit another child, they should just say "Sorry, I have other plans," rather than lying. Just being at home is "another plan"--no further explanation was needed.

24

Define your family's values and standards.

We let them know what we expected of them in ethical behavior and lapses resulted in consequences. We explained that lying, cheating and stealing, even minor, were not acceptable. And we let them know that even if other families' standards were different, we expected them to hew to ours even if "so-and-so does it."

25

Teach them to respect other individuals.

The Golden Rule was basic here and we asked, "Would you like it if someone did that to you?" and "What if everyone did it?" Tougher ethical concepts came later, but basic respect for people and their property started early. And I think respect for others helped develop respect for themselves and their own bodies.

26

Use others' behavior as teaching opportunities.

If you or your child see someone engaging in obviously unethical behavior such as shoplifting or cheating, discuss it, and why it's wrong. Sometimes the excuse, "Everybody does it" provides an opportunity to discuss your family's moral values. If you faced an ethical choice at their age, you can use it as an example and discuss it with your child.

27

Lay the basis for sexual mores.

Even very young children need to learn that their bodies belong to them and should be respected. If they lack this basic concept, tobacco, alcohol, sex and drugs pose even tougher challenges when they reach middle school. We also taught human reproduction in increments as they were age-appropriate, but teaching self-respect and self-care laid the foundation.

28

Teach gratitude as a moral value.

I believe that living with a grateful heart leads to greater happiness, contentment and generosity. We taught our children to recognize the things for which they were grateful and to express their thanks, whether it was saying "thank you" for a kindness or gift or giving thanks to God before dinner. I know that, as adults, my children are grateful.

29

Teach them participation in community service.

We taught our kids that gratefulness includes giving to others, especially those less fortunate than us, and we gave them opportunities to do so. For example, our five-year-old daughter helped me bake and distribute Christmas cookies for the homeless and our son's fifth grade class regularly had lunch with the men of a homeless shelter.

30

Share your religious tradition with them.

All religions provide a code of moral behavior. Although we were raised Christian, my husband and I weren't church-goers until we had children. We decided that returning to church with our kids would help impart our morals, as well as our understanding of the world, including death. If you're religious, no matter your religion, take them to your place of worship.

Teach Your Child to Handle Responsibility

31

Responsibilities add to children's self-esteem.

Sharing in family duties lets your child know he's a valued part of the family. Similarly, sharing in the family's resources through an allowance makes them feel included. For those reasons, we gave our kids chores as soon as they could handle simple ones, but we didn't tie allowance to completion of chores. We used both to emphasize family membership.

32

Responsibilities help prepare them for adulthood.

To be a successful adult, both personally and professionally, you have to be able to fulfill responsibilities and carry through on commitments. Jobs need to be done correctly and on time. This was another reason we gave our kids age-appropriate chores. These responsibilities taught them a lot. They now are very responsible and successful adults.

33

Age and abilities must be considered.

We never expected our children to do chores that were beyond their age and physical capabilities. Clearly, a small child cannot mow the lawn! Chores started with easy ones like picking up toys, bed-making and table setting. Growth and development brought more significant chores. For example, by the time they entered high school they were doing their own laundry.

34

Explain the tasks so he understands.

Whether your child is four or ten, you need to explain why it's important and exactly how to do it. If she doesn't understand what you expect, she can't fulfill your expectations. If our explanations turned out to be unclear, we apologized and tried again. If their performance falls short, explain what's lacking and show them how it's done.

35

Failure to perform should have consequences.

We never withheld allowance for failing to complete chores because allowance reflected family membership, not work done. But sometimes a reprimand and order to "do it now" wasn't sufficient. The result could range from delaying a bedtime story to cancelling a planned outing. This taught them that performance was expected, which was more good training for adulthood.

36

Be consistent in requiring task completion.

If you aren't consistent in requiring that expectations be met, her performance will never be consistent and you will be teaching her that it's O.K. to shirk duties or do a sloppy job. Without learning to do a consistently good job, she'll fail in the working world. We wanted our kids to be hard workers and aim for success, so we were consistent.

37

Resist the temptation to "helicopter" parent.

Sometimes you may think it's easier just to do the job yourself, but resist the temptation. We tried not to "helicopter" parent. We served more as consultants, rather than doing their work or solving problems for them. We never did their homework or school projects for them; we just assisted a little when they asked.

38

Let your child make independent decisions.

Once you've been clear about what results you expect, don't force your child to do the job your way. We wanted our kids to develop independent thought and creative thinking, so we allowed them some leeway in how they accomplished a particular chore. Sometimes they even taught me an easier way of doing things.

39

Teach money management as a responsibility.

At seven years old, our youngest daughter asked what Dad was doing. He said he was paying bills. He explained each one and our assets in simple terms. When she said, "You mean we are *millionaires*?" he quickly showed her what our life cost and how much money was going out, stressing the importance of money management and saving. She still remembers that lesson.

40

Praise them for consistently completing tasks.

With children as well as adults, praise is a powerful motivator when it comes from someone they respect. There's no one whose praise your child values more than yours and that gives you a tremendous teaching assist. We frequently said "good job!" and praised them when they were responsible about doing something.

Help Them Get Along with Others

41

Adult success will require interpersonal skills.

Getting along with others is essential for both a happy life and for success in the adult world and we tried to prepare our kids for that. We started teaching them as toddlers to share their toys and avoid mean words or actions. Later, we encouraged them to solve their own relationship problems but we were always available as consultants.

42

Games teach getting along with others.

We encouraged our kids to learn to get along with others by arranging play dates and encouraging them to participate in games and team sports. Playing games, whether dress-up or *Monopoly*, teaches sharing, taking turns, and playing fair. Getting kids to work together on a fun project is another good teaching method.

43

Encourage them to see both sides.

When our kids were having problems with others, we encouraged them to see both sides of the argument by asking "How do you think he feels?" or "Why do you think she did that?" Gradually they learned that sometimes both sides of an argument have some merit and that compromise is often the best solution. We helped them find compromises.

44

Teach them how to control tempers.

Childhood failure to control temper will lead to yelling and violence, resulting in the loss of friends. Uncontrolled anger as an adult leads to physical abuse, the dissolution of marriages and loss of jobs. Anger control is learned gradually, but you've got to start teaching it early. Starting in toddlerhood, I didn't reinforce tantrums with my attention. That came when the tantrum ended.

45

Help them learn from your example.

Teach anger control by example. Yelling at or hitting a child teaches him that's an appropriate response. If you angrily argue with your spouse or others in front of your kids, they learn it's O.K. and will emulate you. By taking a time-out for myself to prevent disciplining them in anger, I taught them the importance of taking time to cool off.

46

Make sure expectations are age-appropriate.

Toddlers aren't capable of resolving their own disputes and I always had to step in. As our children got a bit older, our expectations about their behavior toward others increased. We let them know bullying was not appropriate and to respect others and their property. We understood shortcomings though, and used them for additional teaching.

47

Be a consultant to your child.

As our kids grew older, we encouraged them to solve their own relationship disputes, but as with all their problem-solving, we were always available as consultants, offering suggestions as to what they might do or say. But we didn't always helicopter in to settle disputes or misunderstandings for them. Solving their own problems gave them confidence they could do it.

48

Let your conflict resolution provide examples.

When they observe you working out disagreements with your spouse or others, they learn from your example. If you faced a similar problem as a child, tell them about it and explain how you handled it. We taught our kids the art of compromise through decisions involving the whole family, like vacations, outings and major family purchases.

49

Don't make them solve being bullied!

Bullying can have major emotional consequences. No matter what the age, if your child is being seriously bullied, you need to step in immediately. Observe and watch for signs that your child is being bullied. Talk to them. If necessary, investigate and take action, by speaking with the other child's parents or going to teachers and school authorities.

50

Praise successful negotiation and conflict resolution.

When your child successfully settles an argument or other relationship difficulty, praise her for it. When they are successful, talk to them about how they handled the problem and why they think it worked. In our family, allowance discussions were another opportunity to teach negotiation. We required a clear rationale for any increase. If we were persuaded, we told them why.

Cultivate Your Child's Creativity and Imagination

51

Creativity increases likelihood of adult success.

Creative problem-solving and innovative ideas are tremendous assets in school and in the adult professional world. In preparing them for success, we encouraged our children's creativity from toddlerhood. Painting and drawing provide a start, but we also responded to some "why" questions with "How do YOU think it works?"

52

Imagination will increase problem-solving skills.

The ability to think "out of the box" helps us solve all kinds of problems, from relationship difficulties to how to build things and, yes, even parenting challenges. We wanted our kids to be good problem solvers so we encouraged them to be creative. There can be many ways to approach a problem. We asked, "What else could you try?"

53

Developing imagination requires some free time.

Children need time to think, to dream and explore, so we provided for that. We limited organized activities like sports and lessons. We also limited screen time. We made sure our kids had time to play and explore on their own. Even preschoolers need thirty-minute periods of quiet time to play with blocks or look at picture books.

54

Playing with others can spur imagination.

When kids play with siblings or friends, their collective imagination increases. For instance, our dress-up closet provided for imaginary characters and plots. It was well-stocked with old Halloween costumes and lots of stuff from Goodwill, such as petticoats, hats, chunks of fur and other costume items that ranged from a Viking helmet to peacock pumps.

55

Encourage them to play "Let's pretend."

Beyond dress-up, pretend play included dolls, puppets, tea parties and putting on plays they scripted and performed. They loved to give us performances after dinner with the raised fireplace hearth serving as their stage. When leftovers accumulated we had "restaurant night" where they made up menus and served us dinner, for which we tipped them a little bit.

56

Find the imagination power in boxes.

Cardboard boxes became train cars for our little guys. Occasionally I picked up cardboard appliance boxes from a local store and, with some creative knife-use on my part, they could become boats, cars, a puppet theater or a small storefront. Turn kids loose with a big box and you never know what they'll turn it into.

57

Building things helps build their imaginations.

Legos, blocks and paper constructions allowed our kids to experiment with building things early on. Older kids wielded hammers to help build Adirondack chairs with dad or a birdhouse with mom. This helped them learn three-dimensional thinking, how things are built and alternative ways of building things. It also gave them a sense of satisfaction.

58

Creative story-telling encourages their imaginations.

One of our eldest daughter's favorite bedtime entertainments was for me to make up stories for her, frequently based on one of the fanciful ponies in her wallpaper border. She also liked to make up stories for me. We encouraged our kids to write and illustrate their own stories. Try reversing roles at bedtime and say, "Tell me a story."

59

Participate in creative play with him.

Playing "let's pretend" with your child is a great way to let them be creative while also providing face time with you. I occasionally took part in the tea parties. Sometimes we took turns with imaginative stories. I would provide the beginning and then say, "What happened next?" and he took a turn telling his part of it.

60

Also introduce them to making music.

Little kids quickly learn how to use simple rhythm instruments and there are some wonderful Kindermusik and other preschool music classes available. We felt that music was a basic part of education, so we required piano classes from kindergarten through fifth grade. They didn't always like it but they learned how to read and make music.

Give Your Child

Mastery of Language

61

They learn language primarily from you.

Parents are much more effective than electronic screens at teaching language or anything else. We always used our adult vocabularies and grammar—no baby talk. Young children quickly pick up word meanings from context and repeated use. We encouraged older kids to ask when they didn't know the meaning of a word and taught them to use the dictionary.

62

Read to them when they're young.

We began with simple stories and simple rhymes and progressed to longer, more complicated stories. They always looked forward to story time and we always made time for it. There is a wealth of good children's literature, so take advantage of it. Read reviews and ask booksellers and friends for recommendations. A love of reading begins before they can read.

63

Read them quality writing and classics.

I always looked for books with good writing, including award winners. Many of the classics--like *Where the Red Fern Grows*, *Little House on the Prairie* and *Little Women*--are classics for good reason. Some classics also allow you to discuss historical periods and how people lived. Don't just take them to fairytale movies-- read the original stories.

64

Let your reading include chapter books.

When I was young my father would read us nightly chapters from books like Robert Louis Stevenson's *Treasure Island* and *Kidnapped*, as well as books by Charles Dickens. We looked forward to each nightly installment and learned how to remember the story from one night to another. I know my facility with language comes from early exposure to good writing.

65

Introduce them to the public library.

Take advantage of your public library and the wealth of kids' books it provides. Libraries often have wonderful story-telling programs for young children. Children's librarians are also a great resource for book recommendations. Library outings with your kids provide them an opportunity to choose their own books. Let older kids have their own library cards.

66

Let them read stories to you.

You can easily increase your child's reading ability and language skills by encouraging them to read stories to you. And don't just give them easy books-- occasionally you can give them something a little more challenging and help them with pronunciation and meanings of new words. Challenging them while being supportive builds their skill and confidence.

67

Don't forget to read them poetry.

Hearing the rhythms and rhyming patterns in poetry helps increase writing ability. I grew up with a *Treasury of Children's Verse* and was encouraged to write my own poetry. I know this also encouraged my language skills. Rhyming patterns also help children remember poems and songs. We included some poetry in our children's reading-aloud menu.

68

Use word plays in daily life.

Our children loved knock-knock jokes and limericks. A favorite, based on Edward Lear, was: *There was a young lady from Ware who rode on the back of a bear. When asked if he trot she said "Certainly not! It's an Emmy-kin-bemikan bear!"* I changed names for each child to "Lizzy-kin" or "Johnny-kin." As they grew, they also loved Dad's puns.

69

Pay attention to grammar and punctuation.

We corrected our children's language mistakes because proper grammar and punctuation count in the professional world. When I worked in the public relations field, good writing skills were essential. When I hired people, I automatically discarded any resume containing grammatical, spelling or major punctuation errors. I didn't want my kids' future resumes to be discarded.

70

Praise her language and writing skills.

When our kids did a good job reading aloud, figuring out a word meaning, or writing a story, we said so. This helped them figure out and recognize good writing. Praising them when they do a good job is the easiest way to reinforce good work. You can point out errors, but give positive reviews.

Introduce Your Child to Scientific Thinking

71

Take advantage of their endless curiosity.

When they asked, "Why?" we explained to them in scientific terms why the rain fell, the sky was blue or where waves came from, etc. With older kids, we encouraged them to investigate for themselves. The *DK Guides* to scientific subjects are wonderful. STEM (Science, Technology, Engineering and Math) abilities are increasingly important today and you can give your kids a head start.

72

Find natural ways of teaching science.

We helped our kids understand biology and respect nature with walks, planting vegetables and watching our pet rabbits deliver babies. We looked for teachable moments when we could explore the whys and hows together. Layering different colors of Jello in a pan, then pushing the firm Jello evenly to one end so it humped and cracked helped them understand how mountains form.

73

Don't wait for middle school projects.

There are lots of fun and easy experiments you can do with young kids. We explained how a plant absorbed water by putting a white flower into water tinted with food coloring, then watching how the flower changed color. Making baking soda and vinegar "volcanoes" was a simple chemistry demonstration. Look online for more science projects for young kids.

74

Visiting museums for kids is fun.

Kids enjoy outings, so take advantage of the ones that offer a little science learning, from dinosaur exhibitions to places like Seattle's Pacific Science Center or similar centers in your area. Look for museums where kids get hands-on experience. When we traveled with kids, we stopped at places that offered something interesting for their age levels.

75

Let them observe development in animals.

The growth of young animals from birth—be it kittens, puppies or farm animals-- fascinates youngsters. Take advantage of local zoos and petting farms. We once raised three ducklings on an ice chest half-submerged in the guest bathtub! We also shared with our kids a wonderful book with photos of embryo and fetal development in human babies.

76

Pay attention to plants and flowers.

Nature walks are great opportunities to explore aspects of science so we hiked with our kids. We observed things like the difference between plants and fungi, how different plants are suited to different conditions and how trees and plants change from season to season and why. Planting flower seeds in a glass jar is a great experiment.

77

Explore the interesting world of insects.

You can order praying mantis and stick bugs; their adaptions and reproduction will fascinate your kids. If you are lucky enough to find a butterfly caterpillar in your garden, snap off the branch it's on and put it in a jar so your kids can observe its change into a chrysalis and then an adult butterfly. Point out interesting bugs.

78

Encourage their reading about scientific subjects.

You'll find lots of science books geared for kids in bookstores, libraries and on Amazon. Again, I can't say enough good about the *DK Guides* which explain with pictures how things are made or how they work. We owned a number of them. Some of the books also offer simple science experiments you can do with your child.

79

Say, "Shall we figure it out?"

When your child asks a scientific question, you often have an opportunity to help her figure things out. As a start, we said, "Why do YOU think that happens?" We encouraged scientific inquiry with books and experiments. None of them became scientists, but it encouraged them to ask "why" and developed their ability to research answers on their own.

80

Teach them how scientific knowledge developed.

We sometimes gave them the history of how scientific knowledge developed, starting with simple things like learning that the world is round, not flat, and that the planets revolve around the sun and not vice versa. This helped them learn that small individual discoveries can eventually add up to major discoveries. Books about historical figures are also helpful.

Cultivate Your Child's Sense of Wonder

81

A sense of wonder is important.

I firmly believe that we should never lose our sense of wonder about the world and all creation. It makes life as an adult richer and makes us more grateful for the world around us. Sometimes as adults we let so-called sophistication stifle our sense of wonder and I think that's tragic. I hope I and my children always retain a sense of awe.

82

Embrace their innate sense of wonder.

Babies are born with an innate sense of wonder about their world. As they grow, embrace their wonder and don't let the "everydayness" of things obscure their—or your—sense of awe about the universe and things in it. We shared awesome experiences like thunder storms, births of animals, telescope star parties with dad, and the Grand Canyon.

83

Wonder helps us experience the divine.

I believe in a divine Creator and wanted our kids to share that belief. Part of that comes from experiencing and being awestruck by the incredible complexity and variety of creation. If we fail to be awed, we don't recognize the tremendous generosity and creativity of our God. Even if kids later become nonreligious, they can retain the awe and gratitude.

84

Explore why they say, "It's cool!"

As kids grow, they frequently express their amazement by saying, "That's cool!" When they said this about natural phenomena, we sometimes asked, "What's cool about it?" This helped them articulate to themselves and us what about the thing or experience inspired their awe. If you elaborate on why it is or how it works, the "coolness" factor can increase.

85

Wonder requires slowing down your pace.

We can't experience the awe in things unless we slow down and look around to see them, appreciating little things like a flower growing through the sidewalk or an amazing sunset. Family hikes, beach visits and vacations offered us great opportunities to relax together, take in the world's wonders and say, "Wow!"

86

Be grateful for all things wonderful.

As I said earlier, gratefulness increases satisfaction, happiness and generosity, especially as adults. Noticing the awesome things in life is the first step—the next is being grateful for them, expressing that gratitude and sharing it with your children. When they express amazement about something in the world, say something simple like, "I'm so glad it's there, too."

87

Don't forget your child is awesome.

One of the things I find amazing in the world is the development of a baby into an adult. The greatest example of this is my own children. That I carried them to birth, watched them grow and mature, and now see them as tremendously loving, creative, generous and successful adults gives me a great sense of awe. They're literally awesome!

88

Praise your child for noticing wonders.

Kids are great at discovering small wonders in the world. Reinforce this by praising them for noticing things: "I'm so glad you noticed that. Isn't it amazing?" Encourage them to see the great and good in the world and compliment them when they do. I think all three of our kids retain their sense of wonder and I'm so glad.

89

Point out the wonders you see.

When I was with one or more children and I saw something that amazed and delighted me, I pointed it out. Each of us observes different things in the world and just as our kids pointed out their observations, I shared mine. It's also teaching by example. When they see you experience and express wonder, they will too.

114

90

Don't ever stifle your child's wonder.

It's easy to stifle a child's sense of wonder by saying, "Oh, that's just because it's that way" or "It's just nature." Factual explanations are really good, but remember to express the "wow" in them. Don't just explain how it works, but also why and how wonderful that is. We encouraged our kids to see the "Wow!" in life.

Remember that Perfect Parents Don't Exist

91

You're absolutely guaranteed to make mistakes.

In child-rearing, as in all else, success involves a lot of trial and error. Some things go wrong no matter how closely you follow guidelines and work at it. If you expect to be a perfect parent, you are doomed to feel like a failure when things don't go right. Don't set unreasonable standards, either for yourself or your children.

92

Perfection's not achievable but greatness is.

Even though you will never be perfect, you can still be a great parent to your child. The things I've talked about are the things that will make you one. If you can succeed in raising an emotionally healthy, happy, generous and loving child, you've succeeded no matter what mistakes you may have made along the way. Great parenting is achievable.

93

Most mistakes have no lasting impact.

Know that most of your mistakes will be minor ones. Losing your temper on some occasions isn't likely to mar you child for life. Don't expect small failures in discipline to deny your child future success. Our son's isolated theft incident didn't set him on a life of crime, even if, on that occasion, he had succumbed to temptation.

94

Forgive yourself for your occasional mistakes.

Because you absolutely will make little mistakes, you need to forgive yourself when you do. When I clearly committed a parenting error, I felt disappointed in myself, but I didn't continue to beat myself over the head with it. If possible, I tried to correct the situation but, even if I couldn't, I always forgave myself and moved on.

95

Apologize when you handle it wrong.

If you subsequently realize that you did or said something to your child that you now regret, apologize to him. Tell him you'll try to do better next time. Expressing your regret will tell your child feel he's still loved. You'll also be doing a great job of modeling for your child how to handle relationship mistakes and the importance of apologies.

96

Look for patterns in your mistakes.

When I made the same mistake twice, I tried to find the reason. For instance, I discovered I was more likely to feel angry when I was frightened, such as by a child who'd wandered away. Fatigue led to bad temper in me, too. Figuring out why I had screwed up made it easier to avoid error in the future.

97

You needn't repeat your parents' mistakes.

The way we parent is initially formed by how we were parented, but it doesn't always have to be that way. If you feel your parents made mistakes in raising you, do it differently. I sometimes blurted out things I had vowed I wouldn't say. I listened for those "parent tapes" and then consciously ignored them.

98

Great parenting will require team work.

You can't possibly be a good parent without help. And sometimes you'll just need a break. The other parent needs to be a strong part of your team. If not, look for extra help from your extended family, neighbors and close friends. My mother-in-law gave me tremendous emotional support. Because grandparents were out of state, an older neighbor became a "grandpa."

99

Sharing with other parents can help.

Sharing your quandaries, questions and frustrations with other parents, including your own, can give you good solutions. You'll also find emotional support in sharing. But always remember that your family and children are unique. Your values may differ from those of your friends. What worked for them may not work for you.

100

Great parenting requires time, patience, humor.

If I had to sum up my parenting advice, it would boil down to being patient with yourself and your child, keep trying, have fun with your child, and keep a sense of humor. Seeing the funny side of a situation puts it in perspective. Always make time for your child. It's the best time investment you'll ever make.

About the Six-Word Lessons Series

Legend has it that Ernest Hemingway was challenged to write a story using only six words. He responded with the story, "For sale: baby shoes, never worn." The story tickles the imagination. Why were the shoes never worn? The answers are left up to the reader's imagination.

This style of writing has a number of aliases: postcard fiction, flash fiction, and micro fiction. Lonnie Pacelli was introduced to this concept in 2009 by a friend, and started thinking about how this extreme brevity could apply to today's communication culture of text messages, tweets and Facebook posts. He wrote the first book, *Six-Word Lessons for Project Managers*, then started helping other authors write and publish their own books in the series.

The books all have six-word chapters with six-word lesson titles, each followed by a one-page description. They can be written by entrepreneurs who want to promote their businesses, or anyone with a message to share.

See the entire *Six-Word Lessons Series* at
6wordlessons.com